Practical Guide to the Operational Use of the HK416

By Erik Lawrence

Printed and bound in the United States of America

First printing 2008
Second printing 2017

ISBN 13: 978-1-941998-82-3
EBOOK – ISBN-13: 978-1-941998-83-0

ATTENTION US MILITARY UNITS, US GOVERNMENT AGENCIES, AND PROFESSIONAL ORGANIZATIONS: Quantity discounts are available on bulk purchases of this book. Special books or book excerpts can also be created to fit specific needs. For information, please contact:

Erik Lawrence   erik@vig-sec.com

Firearms are potentially dangerous and must be handled responsibly by individuals. The technical information presented in this manual on the use of the HK416 reflects the author's research, beliefs, and experiences. The information in this book is presented for academic study only. Neither the author nor the publisher assumes any responsibility for the use or misuse of information contained in this book.

SAFETY NOTICE
Before starting an inspection, ensure the weapon is cleared. Do not manipulate the trigger until the weapon has been cleared of all ammunition. Inspect the chamber to ensure that it is empty and no ammunition is present. Keep the weapon oriented in a safe direction when loading and handling.

AMMUNITION NOTICE
This weapon fires the 5.56x45mm. Firing the incorrect ammunition will damage the weapon and possibly injure the operator.

Training should be received from knowledgeable and experienced operators on this weapons system. Vigilant Security Services, LLC® Training provides this training and continually perfects its instruction with up-to-date information from actual use.

www.vig-sec.com

PREFACE

This manual is intended to be a reference for those involved in the use, maintenance and instruction of the featured firearm. My aim in writing these manuals is to set the record straight and dispel many of the false assumptions related to the different firearms. The early sections of the manual contain background material on the featured firearm which allows the user to gain the basic building blocks for further education. The firearms featured in these manuals have been used for decades by our allies and enemies, and will be for the foreseeable future, so why are we not experts with them? If I am fighting with the firearm or providing instruction on a firearm, I want to use and know their system better than they do.

The rationale for writing these manuals comes from the fact that there are not libraries of easily accessible references to use in developing your own training system for these firearms. Many of the old military field manuals are decades old and were incorrectly translated by someone who had no idea what the firearm could do, let alone basic firearm knowledge. We started from the ground up and developed the manuals to provide instruction in progressive steps that could be easily grasped and continually referred back to. A good grounding in the basics of firearms, safety, and instruction allows the user to use these manuals to their maximum value. A competent user will find little difficulty in interpreting and applying the information in the manual to their own training program.

The guide goes through the most fundamental parts of the firearm in detail and more advanced techniques are not covered as extensively. With this in mind the user can use these principles and adapt it as needed to their required level of instruction. The emphasis of this guide is in acquiring familiarity with the fundamentals of all firearms and learned competence rather than becoming a firearms guru.

Many of the points in these guides were developed from scratch in theatres of conflict and are continually improved and updated for each edition. I have continually used vetted points from users and professionals in the guides to continually update them to the best known practices for each particular firearm. If it is valid and relevant we will include it in the next edition. Please note that this guide assumes some familiarity with the basic concepts in firearm safety, gun handling skills, common sense and an ability to process new information. Readers should have knowledge of the difference in calibers, countries of origin, and the knowledge of the priority of the skills needed for development.

I hope you find this work useful and remember that a manual does not replace proper training and hands on experience. Please email comments to erik@vig-sec.com, particularly if you find any errors or glaring omissions.

Erik Lawrence

Contents

Section 01

Introduction

The objective of this manual is to allow the reader to be able to use the various HK416 variants competently. The manual will give the reader background/specifications of the weapon; instructions on its operation, disassembly and assembly; proper firing procedure; and malfunction/misfire procedures. Operator-level maintenance will also be detailed to allow the reader to understand and become competent in the use and maintenance of the HK416.

Description

The HK416 Series Carbine is a 5.56x45mm lightweight air-cooled, gas-operated, magazine-fed, select-fire shoulder-fired assault rifle. It fires from a closed bolt in either semiautomatic or automatic mode.

HK416A1/A2   CALIBER 5.56X45mm NATO

Model	Weight (no magazine)	Overall Length (closed)	Overall Length (extended)	Barrel Length	Muzzle Velocity
D10RS	7.3 lbs. (3.3 kg)	27 in. (69 cm)	31 in. (78 cm)	10.4 in. (26 cm)	2,540 ft/sec (774 m/sec)
D145RS	7.7 lbs. (3.5 kg)	31 in. (78 cm)	35 in. (89 cm)	14.5 in. (37cm)	2,790 ft/sec (850 m/sec)
D165RS	7.9 lbs. (3.6 kg)	33 in. (84 cm)	37 in. (94 cm)	16.5 in. (42 cm)	2,887 ft/sec (880 m/sec)
D20RS	8.5 lbs. (3.9 kg)	36.5 in. (93 cm)	40.5 in. (103 cm)	20 in. (51 cm)	3,002 ft/sec (915 m/sec)

30-ROUND STEEL HK MAGAZINE *EMPTY* - 0.55 lbs. (0.25 kg)
LOADED - 1.35 lbs. (0.61 kg)

BORE CHARACTERISTICS - Cold hammer forged, hard chrome-lined, six lands

METHOD OF OPERATION - Short-stroke gas-piston operated; rotating bolt

EFFECTIVE RANGE - 600 meters

FRONT AND REAR SIGHT- Comes with HK Diopter sights; Also compatible with all same-plane Picatinny HK416 sights

CYCLIC RATE OF FIRE- 700-900 rounds per minute (rpm)

FIRE CONTROL SELECTION- Safe – Semi-Automatic – Automatic

UPPER RECEIVER- Flat-top full-length Picatinny rail

The barrel rifling twist is 1 turn in 7 inches (1/7), which is necessary to stabilize the SS109 62-grain bullet with steel penetrator used in M855 ammunition when using 16-inch or shorter barrels. The 20-inch barrel variant has a 1 turn in 9 inches (1/9) barrel.

Design

The HK416 uses a proprietary gas-piston system derived from the HK G36. This system was intended to replace and be a reliable upgrade for the direct impingement gas system used by the standard M16/M4. The HK system uses a short-stroke piston driven by gas tapped off the barrel. That gas pushes the operating rod, which contacts the top of the bolt carrier, forcing the bolt carrier to the rear. This design prevents propellant gases from entering the weapon's upper receiver. The reduction in heat and fouling of the bolt carrier group increases the reliability of the weapon, extends the interval between stoppages, and reduces operator cleaning time. An additional benefit for weapon longevity is the reduced stress on critical components due to heat.

NOTE- The buffer in the HK416 should be marked with a red dot. This is a heavier buffer and aids in reliability by slowing down the cyclic rate.

Variants

The Heckler & Koch HK416 is produced in the following variants:

HK416   Standard version (bolt without firing pin safety and without modified barrel extension)

HK416A1   Modified HK416 (bolt with firing pin safety and modified barrel extension)

HK416A2   Modified HK416A1 (with Maritime modifications, Naval Special Warfare requested)

Figure 1-1 HK416A1 D10RS

HK416A1 D10RS

Caliber:	5.56x45mm
Type:	HK Gas Piston System
Barrel Length:	10.4 inches/26 cm
Muzzle Velocity:	2,540 feet/second (774 meters/second)
Length:	Stock closed – 27 inches/69 cm
	Stock extended – 31 inches/78 cm
Weight Unloaded:	7.3 pounds/3.3 kg
Magazine Capacity:	30 rounds

Figure 1-2 HK416A1 D145RS

HK416A1 D145RS

Caliber:	5.56x45mm
Type:	HK Gas Piston System
Barrel Length:	14.5 inches/37cm
Muzzle Velocity:	2,790 feet/second (850 meters/second)
Length:	Stock closed – 31 inches/78 cm
	Stock extended – 35 inches/89 cm
Weight Unloaded:	7.7 pounds/3.5 kg
Magazine Capacity:	30 rounds

Figure 1-3 HK416A1 D165RS

HK416A1 D165RS

Caliber:	5.56x45mm
Type:	HK Gas Piston System
Barrel Length:	16.5 inches/42 cm
Muzzle Velocity:	2,887 feet/second (880 meters/second)
Length:	Stock closed – 31 inches/ 78 cm
	Stock extended – 35 inches/89 cm
Weight Unloaded:	7.9 pounds/3.6 kg
Magazine Capacity:	30 rounds

Figure 1-4 HK416A1 D20RS

HK416A1 D20RS

Caliber:	5.56x45mm
Type:	HK Gas Piston System
Barrel Length:	20 inches/51 cm
Muzzle Velocity:	3,002 feet/second (915 meters/second)
Length:	Stock closed – 36.5 inches/93 cm
	Stock extended – 40.5 inches/103 cm
Weight Unloaded:	8.5 pounds/3.9 kg
Magazine Capacity:	30 rounds

Section 02

Maintenance

Clearing the HK416-style Rifle

1. Ensure the rifle is on SAFE. At all times during the clearing, you must remain aware not to touch the trigger and to keep the muzzle pointed in a safe direction (Figure 2-1). If the safety selector will not rotate to SAFE, the hammer may be in the uncocked position; pull the charging handle to the rear and release. Reattempt to place rifle of SAFE.

Figure 2-1 Safety/selector lever (on SAFE)

2. Remove the magazine by pressing in the magazine release button and pull the magazine downward from the weapon to release it (Figure 2-2). Place the magazine down or in a pouch.

Figure 2-2 Removing the magazine by pressing the magazine release button

3. Extract the cartridge (if any) from the chamber. To lock the bolt open, pull the charging handle rearward, press the bottom of the bolt catch, and allow the bolt to move forward until the bolt catch stops it. Return the charging handle forward. Observe the round extracting and ejecting from the ejection port; do not attempt to retain the round (Figure 2-3).

Figure 2-3 Removing any loaded ammunition from chamber

Clearing the HK416-style Rifle (continued ...)

4. Visually observe that there is no magazine in the rifle and no round in the chamber; physically check with your finger in low-light conditions (Figure 2-4).

Figure 2-4 Inspection of the chamber

NOTE- you must not reverse the steps listed above. If you clear and inspect the chamber prior to removing the magazine, you will load another round into the chamber when you release the charging handle. Always check the safety position and remove the magazine prior to clearing the chamber.

Disassembling the HK416

To insure the proper function of the HK416, it is necessary to disassemble the weapon to inspect and clean the internal components. The names of the parts should be learned through practice in disassembling and reassembling to enhance operator competence. Generally, the parts are named for the functions they perform, i.e., the trigger guard guards the trigger, the charging handle is used to charge the weapon, etc. We have broken down the disassembly into normal operator field strip and detailed armorer disassembly. Stay within your ability level or have a friend who can put your rifle back together.

HK416 type rifle completely disassembled and ready for cleaning and inspection.

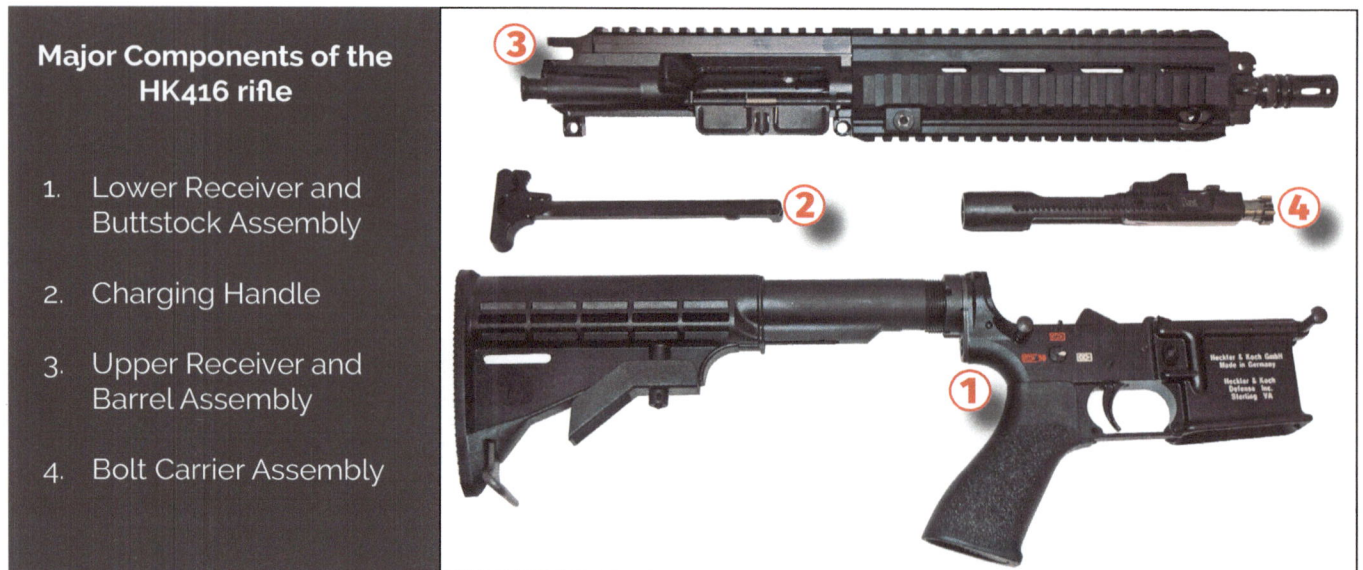

Major Components of the HK416 rifle

1. Lower Receiver and Buttstock Assembly

2. Charging Handle

3. Upper Receiver and Barrel Assembly

4. Bolt Carrier Assembly

Figure 2-5 Major Components of HK416 rifles

To begin the disassembly-

Upper and lower receivers

1. First clear the weapon as per the above description, depending on the weapon's condition.

2. Place the weapon on a flat, clean surface with the muzzle oriented in a safe direction. You may remove the sling if you need to do so, but otherwise you can leave it on the weapon.

3. Separate the upper and lower receivers by grasping the weapon by the buttstock, and with your free hand, push the rear take down pin as far as it will go right; do not force it (Figure 2-6).

Figure 2-6 Separating the upper and lower receivers by pressing the rear take down pin

Figure 2-7 Pushing the pivot pin

4. Push the pivot pin as far as it will go right; do not force it (Figure 2-7). Lay the separated receivers down.

Charging handle and bolt carrier assembly

5. Pull back the charging handle and bolt carrier assembly (Figure 2-8a).

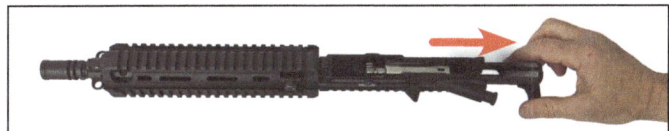

Figure 2-8a Pulling back on the charging handle

6. Lifting the bolt carrier assembly off the charging handle (Figure 2-8b).

Figure 2-8b Lifting out the bolt assembly

7. Pull back and lift out the charging handle (Figure 2-8c).

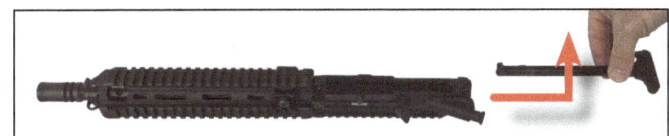

Figure 2-8c Lifting out the charging handle

Components of the Bolt Carrier Assembly

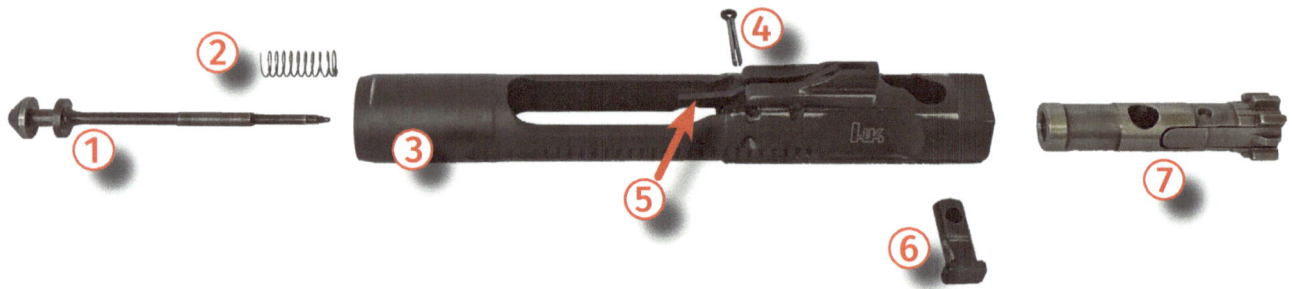

1. Firing Pin
2. Firing Pin Spring
3. Bolt Carrier
4. Firing Pin Retaining Pin
5. Firing Pin Safety
6. Bolt Cam Pin
7. Bolt

Figure 2-9 Components of the bolt carrier assembly

8. Move the bolt assembly forward to the unlocked position and remove the firing pin retaining pin. Do not open or close the split end of the firing pin retaining pin (Figure 2-10a).

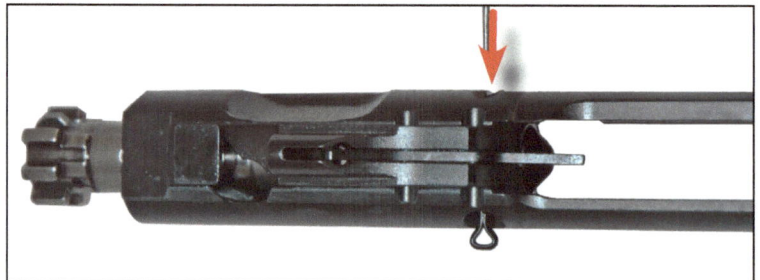

Figure 2-10a Removing the firing pin retaining pin

9. Push in on the bolt assembly to put it in the rearward locked position (Figure 2-10b).

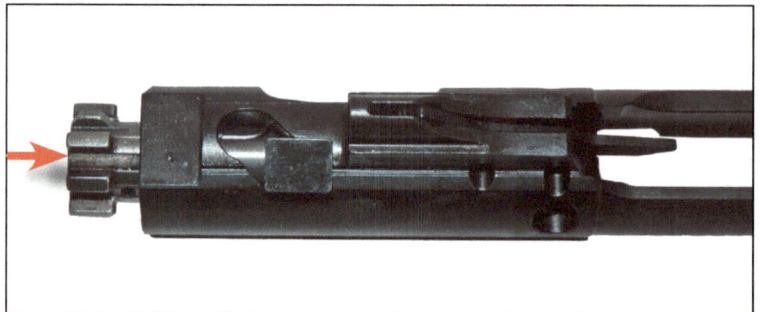

Figure 2-10b Locking the bolt to the rear

10. Remove the firing pin as it drops out of the rear of the bolt carrier assembly; lift on the firing pin safety on the bolt carrier (Figure 2-10c).

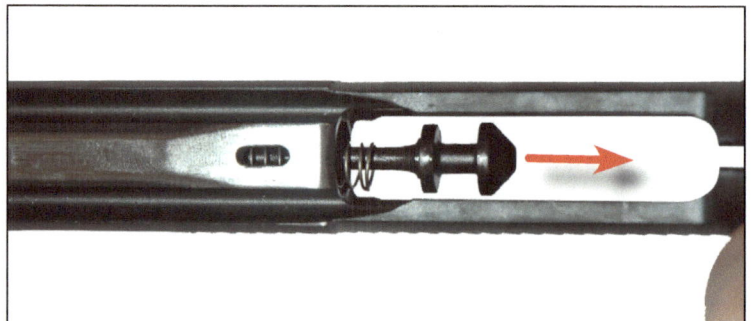

Figure 2-10c Removing the firing pin

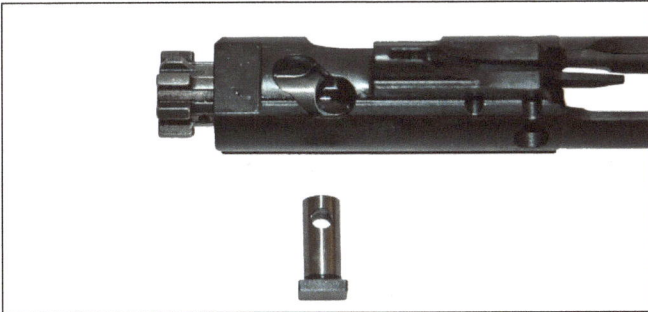

Figure 2-10d Removing the cam pin

11. Give the bolt cam pin (6) a ¼ turn and lift it out (Figure 2-10d).

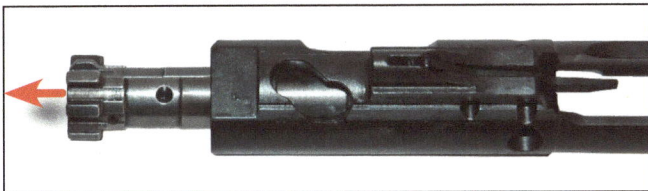

Figure 2-10e Removing the bolt

12. Remove the bolt by pulling it from the front of the bolt carrier (Figure 2-10e).

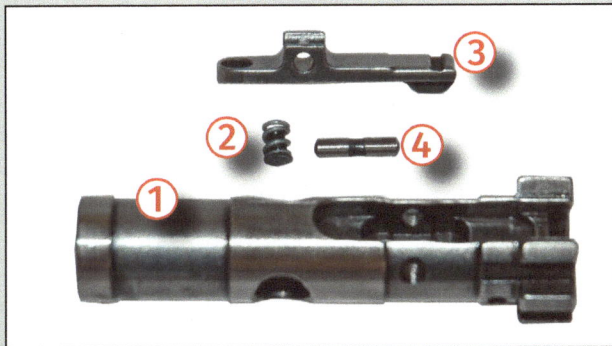

Components of the Bolt

1- Bolt Head
2- Extractor Spring
3- Extractor
4- Extractor Pin

Figure 2-11 Components of the Bolt Head

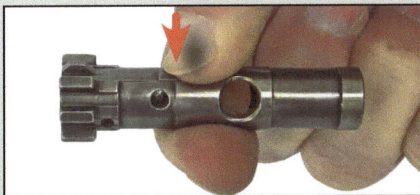

Figure 2-12 Testing extractor spring tension

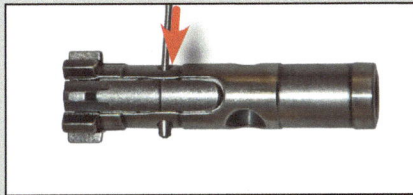

Figure 2-13 Removing the extractor pin

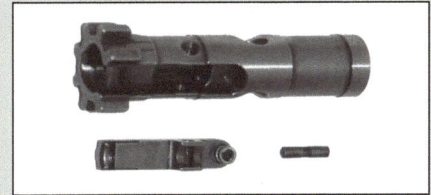

Figure 2-14 Removing the extractor

13. Check the spring tension on the extractor by pressing on rear of it, (Figure 2-12). Extractor claw should return once released. If you are to disassemble the extractor, do it in the following manner.

14. With a punch, cartridge head, or appropriate tool, remove the extractor pin (Figure 2-13).

15. Remove the extractor and spring assembly. Do not remove the spring assembly, its insert, or the O-ring from the extractor (Figure 2-14).

Lower Receiver

16. The hammer must be in the cocked position. Cock the hammer with your thumb if needed. Push in the buffer and depress the retainer to release the buffer (Figure 2-15a).

Figure 2-15a Depressing the buffer spring retainer

17. Remove the buffer. The buffer is under tension, so retain positive control of the buffer as you are removing it from the buffer tube (Figure 2-15b).

Figure 2-15b Removing the buffer

This is the end of the operator disassembly of the weapon.

Prior to any further disassembly, you should seek a qualified gunsmith to instruct you. We list the further disassembly for information purposes only.

Disassembly of the Gas Piston System

Figure 2-16 Loosening the forearm screw

1. Use the bolt head on the bolt carrier to loosen the Free Float Rail System screw, counterclockwise (Figure 2-16).

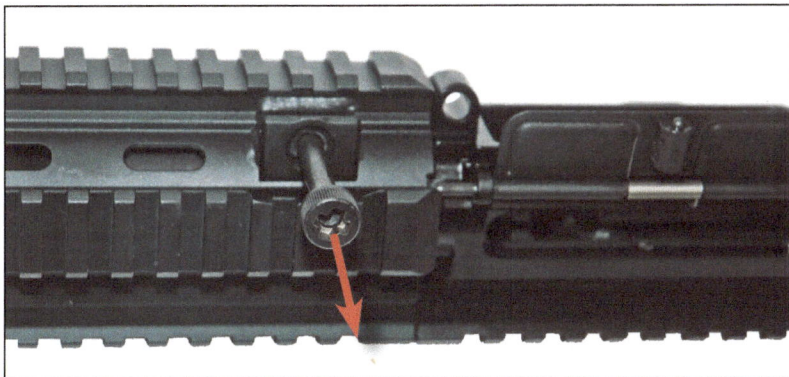

Figure 2-17 Pulling the forearm screw to its retained position

2. Pull the screw to the limit of its travel (Figure 2-17).

Figure 2-18 Removing the forearm from the upper receiver

3. Pull the forearm off the upper receiver (Figure 2-18).

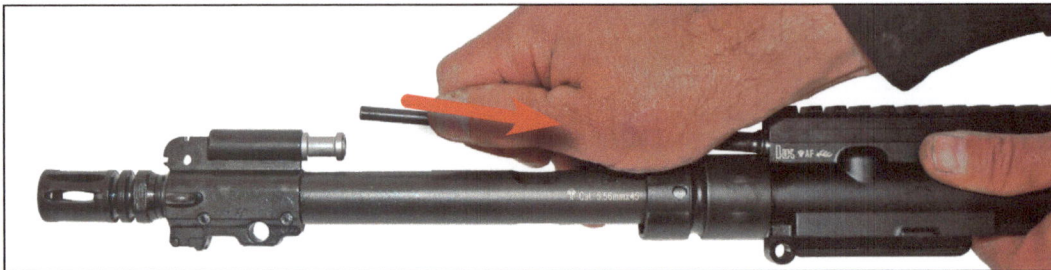

Figure 2-19 Removing the piston rod

4. Pull the piston rod assembly towards the receiver and lift off the gas piston (Figure 2-19).

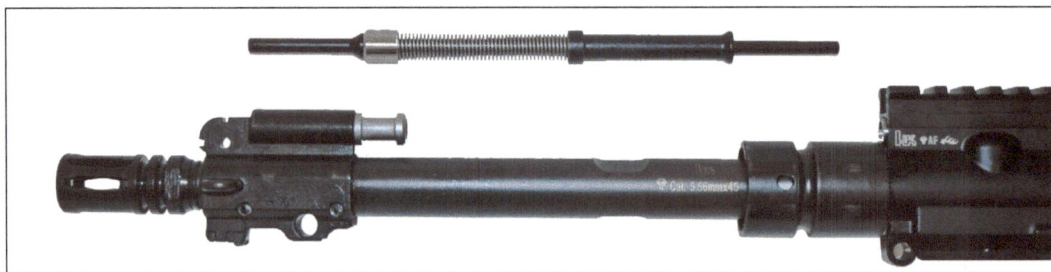

Figure 2-20 Piston rod removed

5. Remove the piston rod assembly (Figure 2-20).

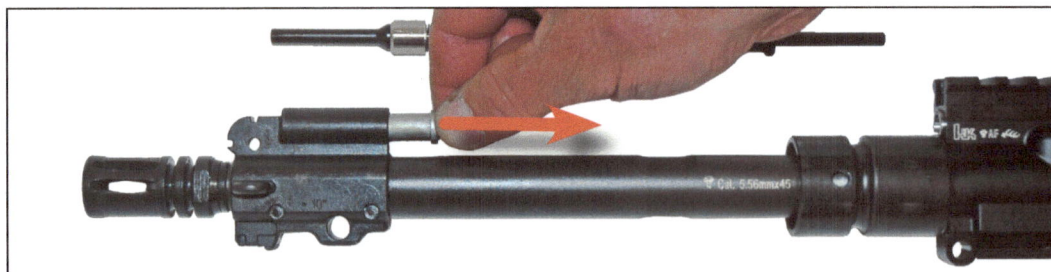

Figure 2-21 Removing the piston

6. Remove the gas piston from the gas block (Figure 2-21).

Figure 2-22 Piston system disassembled

7. Disassembled gas piston system (Figure 2-22).

Cleaning and Lubrication

The HK416 is a dependable rifle, but routine cleaning is advised to insure functionality. Clean the weapon as often as the situation dictates and the environment necessitates. Do not over clean your rifle; keep it serviceable and know how it operates to make effective use of your time.

Keep the weapon free of dirt and dust as much as possible; use a muzzle cap or tape to keep them from entering the bore. Depending on the operating environment, keep lubricant only on metal-to-metal moving parts, and use paint brushes to clean dust and dirt off and out of the weapon.

In hot and humid climates, inspect the weapon often for signs of rust. Keep the weapon free of moisture, and keep a fine coat of lubricating oil on the metal surfaces. If the weapon is exposed to salt air, high humidity, or water, then clean and oil the weapon entirely as often as needed to keep it serviceable.

In hot and dry climates, such as deserts, keep the weapon lubricated only on metal-to-metal moving parts, and use paint brushes to clean dust and dirt off and out of the weapon. Keeping the weapon free of unneeded oil will prevent sand and dust from collecting in the receiver and bore.

Keep your ammunition in containers when not in use, and clean off the cartridges as necessary.

Clean the barrel with the cleaning rod or bore snake. Use solvent-lubricated brass brushes to break up carbon in the bore, and then use a solvent-covered patch to push the carbon out, followed by a dry patch until it is clean. The bores are chrome lined, so they clean up easily. A bore snake is a great bore-cleaning product to use as the barrel is clean with one pass of the bore snake.

Upper Receiver Cleaning

> **Barrel cleaning tips**
> » Clean the bore from the chamber to muzzle direction.
> » Do not reverse the direction of the bore brush while it is still in the bore; push it completely out, and then pull it back through.
> » Use cleaning solvent on the bore and chamber, the gas tube, the upper receiver and barrel assembly, locking lugs, and all areas of powder fouling, corrosion, dirt, or dust.

1. Use a cleaning rod, bore brush, and cleaning solvent to break up initial carbon build-up in bore. Run the rod through the chamber and flash suppressor several times.

2. Assemble the rod and chamber brush for chamber cleaning and break up the carbon in the chamber and lug recesses. Apply cleaning solvent, and insert it into the chamber and lug recesses. Clean by pushing and twisting the cleaning rod.

3. Use the multipurpose brush or bore brush to clean the outside surface of the pro-truding gas tube. Do not use a serviceable bore brush to do this. Do not clean the inside of the gas tube.

4. Once the bore and chamber have been brushed, replace the bore brush with the patch jag, and use the cotton patches to remove the fouling from the bore and chamber area. Change patches unti the bore and chamber are no longer fouled. As with the bore brush, do not change direction until the patch and jag are out of the muzzle.

5. You may have to let the solvent sit on heavily built up carbon deposits. Scraping may be required for built-up carbon.

Bolt Carrier Assembly and Charging Handle Cleaning

1. Clean all parts and surfaces with a general-purpose brush, rag, and/or swab saturated in powder-cleaning solvent.

2. Remove carbon deposits from the locking lugs with a general purpose or bore brush dipped in solvent.

3. Clean under the lip if the extractor; remove all brass shavings.

4. Press the ejector in repeatedly to remove accumulated brass shavings from the ejector hole, and ensure the ejector moves freely. Lubricate it generously. If the spring does not have a noticeable amount of spring tension, replace the extractor and spring.

5. Clean the carbon from the outside surfaces of the charging handle.

6. Clean the firing pin retaining pin and cam pin.

Lower Receiver Assembly

NOTE- Do not use wire-type brushes or abrasive material to clean aluminum surfaces.

1. Wipe and/or brush dirt and sand from the trigger and trigger guard.

2. Wipe and/or brush powder fouling, corrosion, and foreign matter from the lower receiver assembly.

3. Wipe the lower receiver, buffer and buffer spring with a solvent-damp rag.

4. Wipe with a dry rag or use pressurized air to dry the parts.

Inspecting the HK416

To insure an HK416 is serviceable and ready for action, it needs to be inspected periodically and between firings. This inspection can take place while the operator is cleaning the weapon. Disassemble as per the previous section, and organize the parts in groups to be inspected.

Parts to inspect
The overall condition of the weapon and components.

Individual parts
- » Inspect the charging handle for cracks or bends.

- » Inspect the bolt for cracks or fractures, especially in the cam pin hole area. If the bolt needs to be replaced, use a new bolt only. ***DO NOT INTERCHANGE BOLTS BETWEEN RIFLES.***

- » Inspect the firing pin retaining pin for bends, cracks, or dents.

- » Inspect the firing pin for bends, cracks, or a sharp, chipped, or blunted tip. Check firing pin protrusion in bolt with gauge.

- » The gas rings are not removed except to replace them. The gas rings should fit snugly in the bolt carrier, tight enough to support the weight of the carrier. Always replace gas rings as a set. Extend the bolt in the bolt carrier, and set the assembly down on a flat surface; the bolt should remain extended. If it slides into the carrier, you must replace the gas rings as they are too worn to be effective.

- » Inspect extractor for cracks, chips, or wear. Always replace extractor and extractor spring together.

- » When reassembling bolt and bolt carrier, make sure the firing pin retaining pin is inserted behind the large shoulder on the firing pin. If it is inserted in front of the shoulder, the weapon will not fire.

- » Inspect hammer, trigger, and auto sear for chips, cracks, or excessive wear. Replace with new parts if needed.

- » Inspect the lower receiver assembly for a broken or bent trigger, buttstock, corroded or deformed lower receiver, cracked or damaged grip, and bent or damaged safety. Look at the inside parts for cracks, dents, or breaks.

How to Disassemble a HK416 Magazine

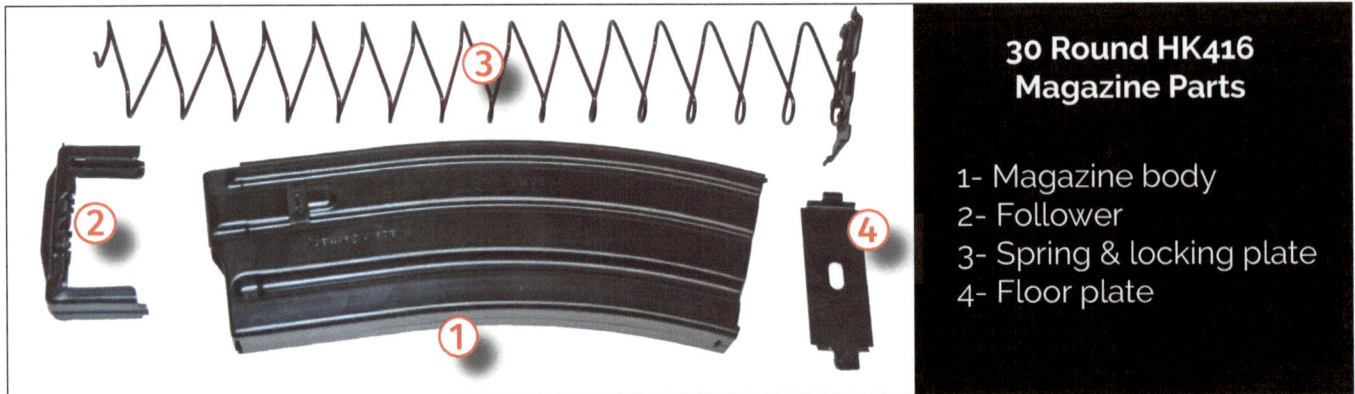

Figure 2-23 Parts of a disassembled 30 round HK416 magazine

To disassemble the magazine, ensure the magazine is unloaded, with no ammo.

1. Use a bullet or pointed object to depress the retaining plate through the floor plate, and start to slide the floor plate to the rear. Be careful not to slide the floor plate fully off until you are ready to apply pressure to the locking plate, as it is under spring tension (Figure 2-24).

Figure 2-24 Magazine floorplate removal

2. Once you have the floor plate started, use your thumb to hold the locking plate and remove the floor plate fully. Now you can release the spring tension in a controlled manner and re-move the spring and follower from the magazine body. The follower and locking plate can be removed from the spring if needed for thorough cleaning.

It is very important to clean the inside of the magazine body and the outside of the follower. Keep the magazine as dry as possible, but lightly coated with a protectant to prevent rust-ing.

To reassemble, just reverse the process.

Lubrication

>> *Do not use any lubricant containing graphite. Graphite can cause corrosion in aluminum alloys.*
>> *Do not use any abrasive cleaners or wire brushes on the upper or lower receivers.*

Lubrication Tips

Figure 2-25 Bolt lubrication points

1. Lightly lubricate the firing pin, firing pin recess of the bolt, outside of the bolt cam pin, and the firing pin retaining pin. Make certain to lubricate the bolt cam pin hole and outside of the bolt (Figure 2-25).

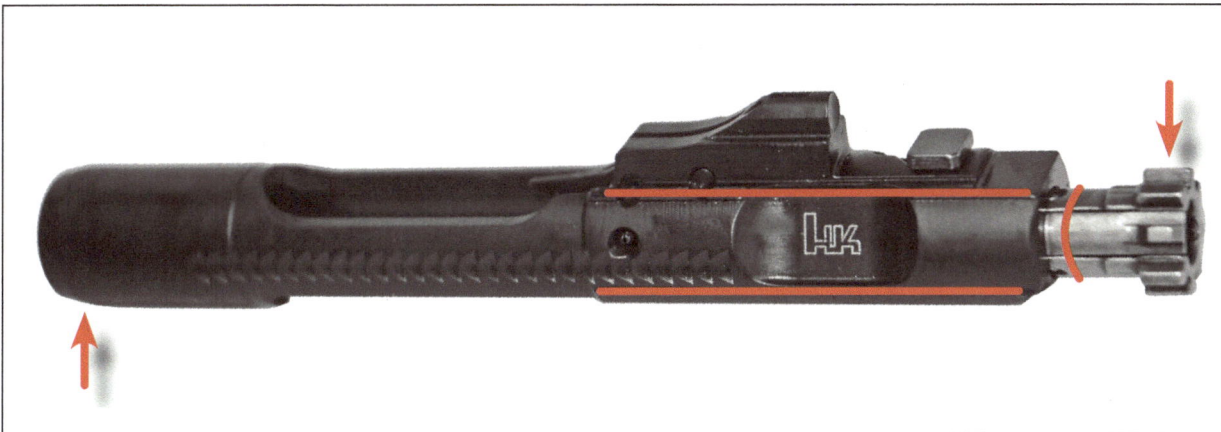

Figure 2-26 Bolt carrier lubrication points

2. Lightly lubricate the inner and outer surfaces of the bolt carrier. Generously lubricate the slide and cam pin area of the bolt carrier (Figure 2-26).

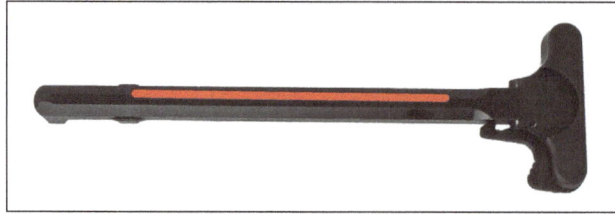

Figure 2-27 Charging handle lubrication

3. Lightly lubricate the charging handle (Figure 2-27).

Figure 2-28 Piston and piston rod lubrication

4. Lightly lubricate the gas piston and gas piston assembly (Figure 2-28).

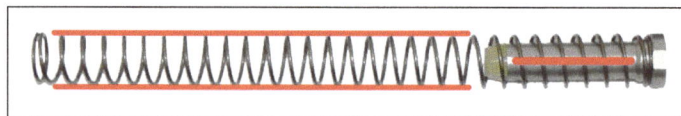

Figure 2-29

5. Lightly lubricate the recoil spring and buffer (Figure 2-29).

Figure 2-30 Takedown and pivot pin lubrication

6. Lightly lubricate takedown pins and the inside parts of the lower receiver (Figure 2-30).

7. Lightly lubricate the bore and chamber with a lightly lubricated patch on the cleaning rod.

8. Lubricate the locking lugs on the bolt.

Firearm-specific cleaners and lubricants are best to use. However, spray carburetor cleaner is very useful for removing carbon buildup in the upper receiver and bolt carrier assemblies. In areas where weapon-specific cleaners and lubricants cannot be obtained, testing by Rock Island Arsenal has found that Automatic Transmission Fluid can be safely used as a cleaner and light lubricant. Also, 20-weight synthetic motor oil can be used as a lubricant with no harmful effects to the weapon.

Lube all operating parts. Inside the receiver, go ahead and coat the metal in a light film of CLP or light machine/gun oil. Some types of grease TW-25B can be used on the metal-to-metal (shiny spots) to allow the rifle to operate smoothly.

Protection

Use a type of Cleaner/Lubricant/Protectant (CLP). When not available, some prefer motor oil, automatic transmission fluid, or light gun oil. With a rag, wipe down all exposed metal with CLP, interior and exterior, parkerized, blued, or otherwise. A slight film is all that is required to protect the gun.

Assembling the HK416

As you are assembling the HK416 rifle, re-inspect the internal parts to ensure that each is in working order.

Lower Receiver Assembly

Figure 2-31 Inserting the buffer and buffer spring into the stock tube

1. Insert the buffer and buffer spring into the buffer tube and push past the buffer re-taining pin (Figure 2-31).

Bolt Carrier Assembly and Charging Handle

2. Extractor- If the extractor spring comes loose from the extractor, seat the large end of the extractor spring in the extractor. Ensure the reinforcement ring is around the spring. Insert the extractor with spring assembly into bolt. Push extractor until the holes on the extractor and bolt are aligned, and insert the extractor pin.

3. Slide the bolt assembly into the bolt carrier, far enough to insert the cam pin.

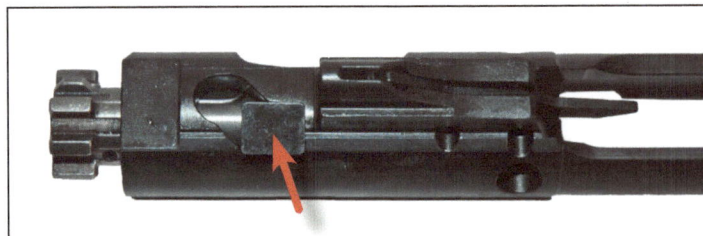

Figure 2-32 Inserting the cam pin

4. Insert the bolt cam pin and give it a ¼ turn (Figure 2-32).

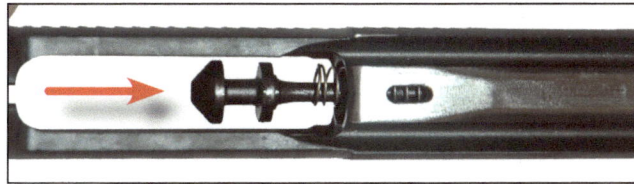

Figure 2-33 Inserting the firing pin with its spring on it

5. Drop the firing pin into its opening in the back of the bolt, and press up on the firing pin safety to allow it to fully seat (Figure 2-33). Ensure you have the firing pin spring on the front of it prior to insertion.

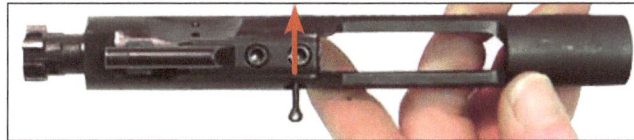

Figure 2-34 Inserting the firing pin retaining pin

6. Pull the bolt assembly forward and insert the firing pin retaining pin in the area behind the large flange of the firing pin (Figure 2-34).

7. Turn the bolt carrier assembly up and try to shake out the firing pin. The firing pin must not fall out. If the firing pin does fall out, remove the firing pin retaining pin, reinsert the firing pin fully, and reinsert the firing pin retaining pin. Recheck for proper assembly; the weapon will not fire with the retaining pin not properly holding in the firing pin (Figure 2-35).

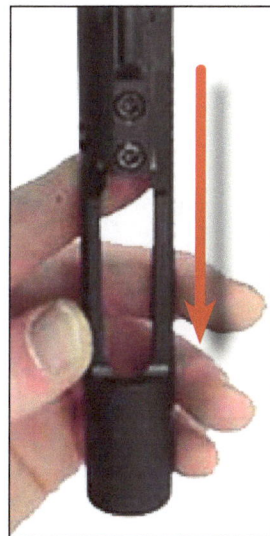

Figure 2-35 Ensuring firing pin is retained

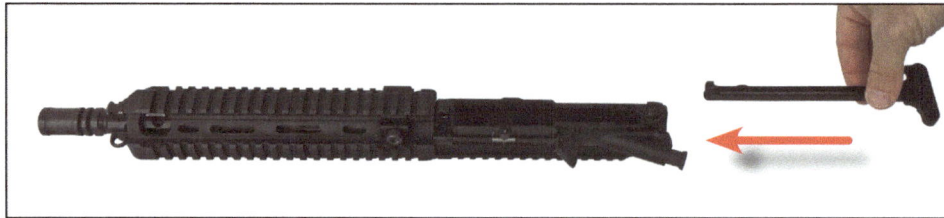

Figure 2-36 Placing the charging handle into the top of the receiver

8. Place the charging handle into the upper receiver and engage the handle's lugs with the track in the receiver; then push the charging handle part way into the upper receiver (Figure 2-36).

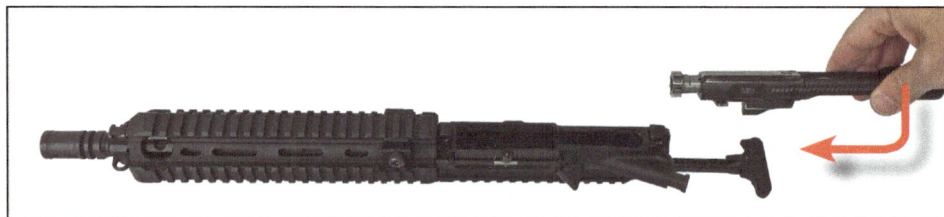

Figure 2-37 Inserting the bolt carrier group

9. Slide the bolt carrier assembly, bolt extended, into the upper receiver (Figure 2-37).

10. Push the charging handle assembly and bolt carrier assembly together into the upper receiver.

Figure 2-38 Aligning and pressing the pivot pin in

11. Align the upper and lower receivers. Align the pivot pin holes with the pivot pin and push the front pivot pin in. Note that the hammer must be in the cocked position; press it down with your thumb to cock (Figure 2-38).

Figure 2-39 Closing the receivers and pressing in the takedown pin

12. Closing the upper and lower receivers. Push in the rear takedown pin (Figure 2-39).

Figure 2-40a Sliding the forearm over the barrel

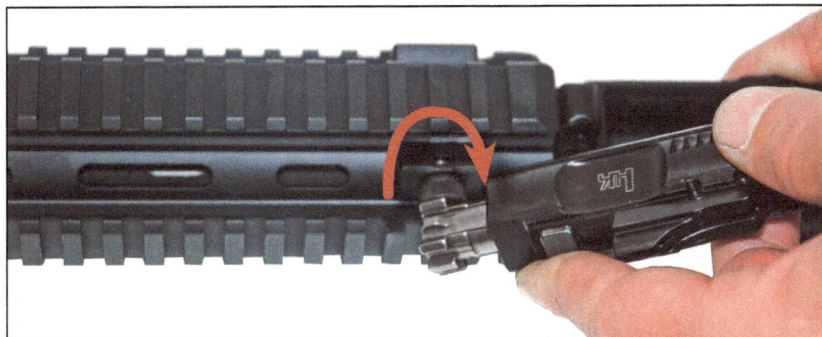

Figure 2-40b Tightening the forearm retention crossbolt screw

13. If your forearm was off, then reattach the forearm and tighten the crossbolt screw (rightie tightie) if you removed it during disassembly (Figures 2-40a & 240b).

Function Check Procedures

» Place the weapon on FIRE.

» Pull the charging handle to the rear and return it to its forward position.

» Place the weapon on SAFE.

» Pull the trigger; nothing should happen.

» Place the weapon on the semi-automatic selector position.

» Pull the trigger, and the hammer should release; hold the trigger back.

» Pull the charging handle to the rear and release; let up on the trigger and press it to release the hammer again. Note that you hear the reset.

» Pull the charging handle to the rear and release, and place the weapon on the automatic-selector position.

» Pull the trigger, (hold the trigger back) and the hammer should release.

» Pull the charging handle back, let up on the trigger, and you should not hear any hammer movement.

» Pull the charging handle to the rear, and return it to its forward position.

» Place the weapon on SAFE.

HK416 Ammunition Magazines

The weapon is fed by the new HK High Reliability steel magazines and standard M4 aluminum magazines (Figures 3-1 and 3-2). Standard HK magazines are designed to hold 30 rounds for the HK416.

Loading the Magazine

Ensure you have 5.56x45mm ammunition; this ammunition is easily confused for with 5.45x39mm (AK74). Inspect it for uniformity, cleanliness, and serviceability. Check all for undented primers, and use only issued ammunition.

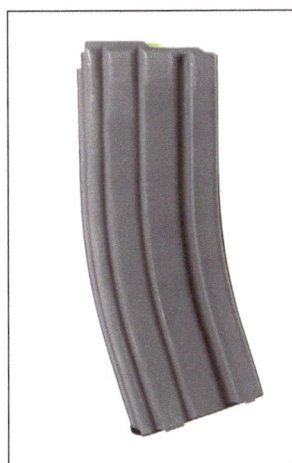

Figure 3-1 Standard 30-round aluminum magazine

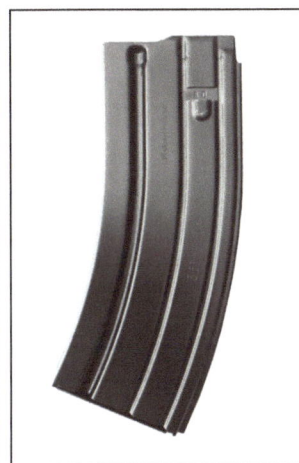

Figure 3-2 HK High Reliability 30-round steel magazine

1. Use your non-dominant hand to hold the magazine with the front of the magazine toward your fingertips. With your dominant hand, one at a time, place the cartridge over the top of the magazine follower between the feed lips, and press the cartridge straight down until it snaps under the feed lips. Once the cartridge is under the lip of the magazine body, slide it fully to the rear so the next round will be allowed to be pushed down (Figure 3-3).

2. The magazine can hold 30 cartridges (the 30th round will be on the top right as looking down on it); load 29 (the 29th round will be on the top left as looking down on it), and then load the chamber so you have 28 in the magazine and one in the chamber and just 29 rounds in magazines you load in your pouches. It is easiest to lay out the number of rounds for each magazine so you don't have to count the rounds as you load the magazine.

Figure 3-3 Magazine hand loading procedure

Loading the HK416 Rifle

NOTE: Keep the weapon oriented in a safe direction.

Clear the weapon as described in the previous section.

Loading from the open bolt

1. Lock the bolt to the rear. Pull the charging handle to the rear, press in on the lower portion of the bolt catch, and then release the rearward pressure on the charging handle and return it forward to its locked position. Once the bolt is locked to the rear, place the safety, located on the left-hand side of the weapon, to the (SAFE) position, (Figure 3-4). **NOTE-The weapon will not go onto SAFE if the hammer is not cocked.**

Figure 3-4 Locking the bolt to the rear

2. Insert the top of the magazine into the magazine well (bullets towards end of muzzle), and press the magazine upwards to lock it in (Figure 3-5a).

   Ensure it is locked into place by tugging down on it (Figure 3-5b). Do not force your magazines into the lower receiver by loading 30 rounds and ramming it into a rifle with the bolt forward.

Figure 3-5a Inserting the magazine into the rifle

Figure 3-5b Ensuring the magazine locked into the rifle

3. Depress the upper portion of the bolt catch to release the bolt (Figure 3-6). Listen for the chambering of the round while you watch the ejection port.

Figure 3-6 Chambering a round

Loading from the closed bolt

1. Insert magazine until magazine catch engages. Pull down slightly to assure proper lock up. Do not force or pound the magazine into the receiver. A fully loaded magazine may not want to lock into the magazine catch; one round should be removed to allow for proper lock up. I suggest 28-round magazines.

Figure 3-7a Inserting the magazine into the rifle

Figure 3-7b Ensuring the magazine locked into the rifle

2. Pull the charging handle fully back and release. As the bolt travels forward by the weapon's spring tension, it will strip the top round from the magazine and force it into the chamber (Figures 3-7a, 3-7b and 3-7c). It is a good habit of tapping the forward assist to ensure the bolt is fully forward and in battery. Riding the charging handle will not allow for the bolt to return to battery.

Figure 3-7c Charging the rifle

3. If you are preparing the rifle to fire, it is now ready; otherwise, ensure the selector is in the SAFE position (Figure 3-8). Keep the safety on SAFE until you have the intention to shoot.

Press Check procedure

To check if the chamber was loaded with a round, with the safety still engaged, pull the charging handle back slightly to see the casing being pulled from the chamber.

Figure 3-8 Safety/Selector on SAFE

Once you have seen or felt the casing in the chamber, return the charging handle forward and tap the forward assist to ensure the bolt is in battery. In low light, you may have to reach in and feel the cartridge casing to ensure the chamber is loaded.

Cycle of Function

Shooters can recognize and correct stoppages when they know how the HK416 Rifle functions. Each time a round is fired, the parts of the weapon function in a cycle or sequence. Many of the actions occur at the same time.

These actions are separated in this manual only for instructional purposes.

1. The semi-automatic cycle is started when the trigger is pulled. The sear is rotated forward and down, releasing the hammer. The hammer then rotates forward and strikes the firing pin. After firing, the bolt moves to the rear, rotating the hammer back toward the cocked position. The disconnector catches the hammer and holds it to the rear until the trigger is released. This action allows the sear to rotate back and engage the hammer and hold it in the cocked position for the next shot. The function of the disconnector is to make certain that another round cannot be fired until the trigger is released and pulled again.

2. The full-automatic cycle is started when the trigger is pulled. The sear is rotated forward and down, releasing the hammer. The hammer then rotates forward and strikes the firing pin. After firing, the bolt moves to the rear, rotating the hammer back toward the cocked position. The auto sear notch on the hammer catches on the auto sear and holds the hammer in the cocked position. As the weapon completes its cycle during the last 1/2" of movement of the bolt carrier, the bolt carrier engages the auto sear and rotates it forward and down, releasing the hammer and starting the cycle again. This cycle continues until the trigger is released or the ammunition supply is exhausted.

3. The sequence of functioning is as follows:

    A. **Firing**. When the trigger is pulled, the hammer rotates and strikes the back of the firing pin where it protrudes from the back of the bolt. This action drives the firing pin forward, and the tip of the firing pin protrudes through the firing pin hole in the bolt face and strikes the primer of the cartridge, and the primer fires the cartridge.

    B. **Unlocking**. After the cartridge is fired and the bullet passes the gas port, some of the expanding gases go into the gas block and from there, to the gas cylinder, forcing the piston to the rear. As the piston drives the bolt carrier to the rear, the cam surface engages the bolt, and it is rotated 45 degrees counter-clockwise, unlocking the bolt.

    C. **Extracting**. Extracting begins during the unlocking cycle. The rotation of the bolt loosens the cartridge case in the chamber. As the bolt and bolt carrier move to the rear, the extractor pulls the cartridge case from the chamber.

    D. **Ejecting**. As the cartridge case is pulled from the chamber, the bolt passes by the ejector. The extractor grips the right side of the cartridge case and causes it to spin form the weapon as it reaches the ejection port.

E. **Cocking**. As the bolt carrier moves to the rear, it engages the hammer and rotates it back to the cocked position. At the same time, it compresses the operating spring.

F. **Feeding**. As the bolt starts its forward movement, it engages the rim of the next cartridge in the magazine. It then pushes that cartridge forward, and the cartridge is aligned with the chamber by the cartridge guide as the base of the cartridge clears the magazine feed lips.

G. **Locking**. As the cartridge is chambered, the bolt enters the barrel trunnion. As the cartridge is full chambered, the extractor snaps over the rim of the case. As the bolt carrier continues forward, the cam surface engages the bolt, and the bolt is rotated 45 degrees clockwise, locking the bolt into the trunnion, and the weapon is ready to be fired again.

Firing the HK416

Orient toward the desired area/target, take a proper sight alignment and sight picture, rotate the selector/safety lever (from the SAFE position) to the desired fire position (first rotational position stop is for SEMI-AUTOMATIC and the second rotational position stop is for FULL-AUTOMATIC), and press the trigger straight to the rear without interrupting your sight alignment and sight picture.

Once your target engagement is complete, rotate the selector to the SAFE position.

Section 04

Performance Problems

Malfunction and Immediate Action Procedures

Malfunctions are usually preventable through good practices, but they may still occur out of the blue from time to time. Of course, you hope it is on the practice range, but you should treat each one as if you are in a life-or-death situation. Practicing proper and effective corrective actions will allow you to be more confident in your rifle handling. In stressful situations, you can become much more stressed due to an unforeseen malfunction that is easy to correct.

You should always practice taking a covered position to correct malfunctions with considerations on how you operate.

Most problems are often attributed to incorrect operator use or maintenance, faulty ammunition, and/or problems in the rifle. The magazine is the culprit most of the time, so the magazine must be inspected. Each magazine needs an identifying mark. If the same problem exists with more than one magazine, then more than likely it is a rifle, operator, or ammunition problem.

Stoppage
A stoppage is a failure of an automatic or semi-automatic rifle to complete the cycle of operation. The operator can apply immediate or remedial action to clear the stoppage. Some stoppages that cannot be cleared by immediate or remedial action could require weapon repair to correct the problem. A complete understanding of how the weapon functions is an integral part of applying immediate-action procedures.

Immediate Action
This involves quickly applying corrective actions to reduce a stoppage based on initial observation or indicators, but without determining the actual cause. To apply immediate action, the operator would perform these steps:

» Lightly slap upward and tug downward on the magazine to ensure it is fully seated and locked.

» Pull the charging handle fully to the rear and check the chamber (observe for the ejection of a live cartridge or expended casing).

» Release the charging handle, allowing it to shut by the force of the buffer spring (do not ride it forward).

» Hit the forward assist assembly to ensure the bolt is in battery.

» Attempt to fire the rifle.

NOTE- Apply immediate action only one time for a given stoppage; do not apply immediate action a second time. If the rifle fails to fire after the performance of immediate action, then clear the weapon and inspect it to determine the cause of the stoppage or malfunction and take appropriate remedial action.

Remedial Action

Remedial action is the continuing effort to determine the cause for a stoppage or malfunction and to try to clear the stoppage once it has been identified.